19 POEMS

from Vero Beach

By Anna M. Figueroa

Title: 19 Poems (from Vero Beach)

Author: Anna M. Figueroa

Copyright ©2025 by Anna M. Figueroa

All rights reserved.

No part of this book may be reproduced, distributed, or transmitted in any form or by any means, including photocopying, recording, or other electronic or mechanical methods, without the prior written permission of the publisher, except in the case of brief quotations embodied in critical reviews and certain other noncommercial uses permitted by copyright law.

For permission requests, write to the publisher at the address below.

Published by Pine Tree Press

www.pinetreepress.com

Printed in USA

19 POEMS *from Vero Beach*

DEDICATION

This book is dedicated to my mother and all her dreams, those realized and those unrealized.

It is also dedicated to Dr. Orlando Gutierrez Boronat, my life-long friend, who has encouraged me, provided constructive criticism, and that which I needed most...courage.

TABLE OF CONTENTS

Introduction 9

Twilight, Stars and Station Wagons 16

Burn 19

I Owe You a Poem 20

Hands 26

A Woman Alone 29

The Words 33

Missed 37

Now 40

All I Am 42

Love Letters 46

After 50

Tequila 53

Woman of Jerusalem 44

What of You 61

The Palestinian 50

Fly 68

Through the Smoke 71

Unwritten 75

Stay With You (for Enzo) 59

Being 82

Not Forever 85

Midnight	*88*
Julio's Stride	*91*
R&B	*94*
Autumn	*97*
New Orleans	*100*
Gently	*103*
Rage for Silence	*105*
Twilight Dance	*108*
Chasing Shade	*112*
Tres De La Tarde En La Ciudad (Sentada, Esperando Las Cinco)	*114*
Nos Queda	*118*
Mi Poder	*121*
La Habana	*125*
Cuando te Vayas	*129*
Caída	*133*

ACKNOWLEDGMENTS

I would like to acknowledge and thank my son, Julio Mendez, Jr., for always reminding me that it is never too late to be happy.

I also want to thank my dear friend Maria Rivero, who was the first person to ever read my first book. After spending an entire afternoon reading my novel and continually throwing me out of my own office, she told me she was not a big reader but that she could not put it down…the highest of compliments.

Lastly, I want to thank my high school English teacher, Brother Carl Shonk, who taught me to go beyond the words to find meaning.

INTRODUCTION

Poetry, good, beautiful, and true poetry, is always a heroic act. It is steadfast resistance to the fragility of time, to the happenstance of circumstance, to the grind of being, to entropy itself.

Poetry is a heroic act because it dares to go beyond the usual, or rather into it, in order to demonstrate that the "usual" doesn't exist. That each life, each chord, each vibration which rises out of humanity to flow with the permanent, the eternal, dares to challenge the world.

Poetry is sight. A very special kind of sight. The one who tries to perceive things as they are and not as they appear to be. The deep sight, the sight of the soul, which sees into the chaos, and then must strive to show the world that there is a fundamental connection between all things. That there is a rhythm, a pattern, a synchronicity to life which the words of poetry not only evoke but make you vibrate with.

Poetry is lines on paper backed up by a life lived in pursuit of the highest sensitivity. To find the harmony underlying both joy and suffering, love and struggle, growth and death, and time.

Poetry is an echo… which demonstrates that all of being, across time, is in tune with what words can show, but also that words take on life and dance across the ages.

My friend Anna Figueroa is heroic; she has sight, she is a poet.

Anyone who confronts life in the world with the conviction that they will live as they think, that they will think in pursuit of truth, and that they will not silence what they consider to be true, is heroic. Heroism is nothing but the rigorous, devoted, and applied study of the highest levels of love. And that's Anna and her life and her poetry.

I don't know when the sad moment was when poetry and philosophy divorced, probably as another symptom of the failings of the modern world, which must compartmentalize everything in order to deal with its own insecurities. However, poetry and philosophy are undoubtedly and inextricably woven together as part of the life action that takes us out of the mud and towards the stars. Poetry and philosophy are one in this book.

What is exceptional about Anna Figueroa is that she has faced a life of challenges: the eldest of five siblings born to exiled parents, attaining a college education while working full time, a divorced mother raising a son, a successful entrepreneur, a community activist, a cancer survivor, and stubbornly persistent in her faith in Jesus Christ. And that life of nonstop struggle she has managed to transmute, through and with her pen, into a written beauty that transcends the multiple veils of the day-to-day, in order to show the universal beauty, the universal rhyme and reason, inherent in each moment of existence in this realm of ours: the metaxy.

Anna's "19" does that. It spans the intersection of being, from the body to the mind and the spirit, across relationships, issues of gender and sex, questions posed to God, and the interplay with nature and identity. It is a book about the courage it takes to be a woman, to face life, to question beyond the immediate, to engage in dialogue with God.

Thus, in a classical sense, it is a complete work. I think that it is a complete work that will transcend its time inasmuch as the good, the true, and the beautiful are eternal. But it is also a complete book of poems about the uniqueness of Miami, about a culture and a people, a city within a city, the persistent observation of which leads to the discovery of certainties applicable and pertinent to the human soul anywhere and everywhere. Precisely because Anna is very much Cuban, very much American, and very much Miami. Her moment will not be repeated; it is unique, it has no substitute.

Anna Figueroa has much to say. It's time for America to begin to listen to her Cuban American symphony of letters.

Dr. Orlando Gutierrez Boronat.

Years ago, going through some of my aunt Ibis' papers after her passing, I found a scrap of paper with a phrase written on it in her handwriting. It read, "Todo amor, como todo arte, tiene sus raíces en el dolor." In English, it means all love, like all art, has its roots in pain.

I don't agree that all of it must come from pain. Sometimes, joy can be the most creative force of all, but pain makes us dig deep into ourselves and root out that which we often ignore when we are content. I find that writing it all down helps me understand it and, occasionally, to find acceptance and peace.

Poetry is how we reach for the divine, to that which is beyond the experience itself… that which gives meaning to it all somehow. In the creation of the poem, we turn the moment into art. Whether the moment is filled with love, anguish, or confusion, poetry allows it to be seen through the soul instead of only the mind. Poetry, like all art, is subject to the beholder. The reader may interpret something completely different than what the author meant to convey, and that, in my view, is also art.

I don't know how poetry comes to others. I only know how it comes to me. Poetry, for me, is a verbal snapshot of a moment or a feeling in my life. Sometimes it is extremely personal, a way to process what is happening to me and my feelings about it. Other times, it is a snapshot of something I have observed or something shared with me that moves me. It is my way of describing what I see in my mind's eye in the moment. I just know that the words come, often in a rush. I know that they need to be on paper. So, I write.

Some of these poems are about me, or past versions of me. Others are about people I care about, and some are about strangers whom I crossed paths with for a brief time, who made me feel something that, to me, is important. All of them are my word paintings. They are my way of capturing the rush of words and feelings that come, sometimes uninvited but always welcome.

I hope you enjoy them and that they make you feel something, too. I thank you for the gift of your precious time as you read them. It means the world to me.

Anna M. Figueroa

***19 POEMS** from Vero Beach*

Twilight, Stars and Station Wagons

I lay on that station wagon hood,
knees bent, arms spread wide,
watching the beautiful splashes of color in the sky,
yellow, orange, pink and purple,
fading and slowly turning into a dark, new canvas.
Staring up at the millions of stars in the southwestern sky,
dreaming of the life that I knew I would lead,
a life of writing stories from some charming Parisian café,
stories about love and broken hearts and heroes.
Staring at those divine lights,
until I became so dizzy, I thought I would fall…
feeling I was falling off more than just that hood.
Falling off the very edge of the world.
Not understanding that in the end,
that is what life would become.
Falling. Lights. Beauty. Dizziness.
A broken heart.
Shattering and mending and then breaking again.
I didn't know the stars held so much darkness and texture.
I just saw their light and felt their dust enter my childish heart.
There are no stars in the sky above me now,
but there is stardust threaded through the cracks inside me.
I comfort myself, knowing that it will seal the wounds of my soul,
like divine water and gravel,
helping me to stay balanced,
as the world tilts around me
and the sky shimmers.

19 POEMS *from Vero Beach*

Burn

The manicured, softly treaded path,
always stretching there before me,
never enticed me.
These rebel feet always refused to move forward there.
The easy shade and smooth, cold stepping stones,
laid out so carefully,
ever meant for someone else.
In the end, I always chose
the rocky, steep cliffs
where reasonable women do not willingly wander.
The places where fierce, magnificent dragons
hid their golden treasures in dark, purple caves.

In the end, I always wanted the magic of the fire-breathers.

So many good and gentle loves
have tried to reach my stubborn heart.
Loves that would have made my journey warm and sheltered.
Men of honor who would have fought the monsters for me.
This foolhardy, wild heart inside of me wanted to write stories
in which I was the hero,
rescuing instead of being rescued.

In the end, I wanted to love the monsters instead of fighting them.

Resting occasionally in the cool streams I came upon,
as life and time pushed me along,
it was not enough.
Always, I stepped away, reaching for the sun's heat.
The burn making me feel alive,
the heat filled not only with uncertainty
but also brimming with adventures.
The blaze reminding me,

that life should never be regretted.
In the end, I chose fire.

Now, the cliffs and the dragons and the fire of the sun
all swirl and dance inside me.
Now they course through my veins.
Now I understand,
that I *am* the cliffs and the dragon and the fire.

I Owe You a Poem

Dear friend,
I owe you a poem.

You, who have made me remember
that deep down, I am a poet.
You, who remember the girl I used to be.
I owe you a poem.

Was there poetry in me back then?
I don't know, but if there was,
it was probably unsure and unsteady,
like a newborn wild thing.
Yet, even then,
we knew each other
a bit, didn't we?

Now we know each other differently.
Now, you know my poems
and now, I know the warrior in you.
Now, we are friends who see
each other differently,
more clearly and reverently.

For you, who has helped me to remember
who I am supposed to be.
I hope that I remind you
of all you are meant to be
every so often, dear friend.
I owe you a poem.

You, who cheer me on.
You, who believe
that there are great stories inside my heart.
What a true friend you are!

I owe you a poem.

You, who shares ideas
as easily as others share gossip.
You, who makes me think and
search the meaning of unfamiliar, beautiful words,
discovering their meanings
just as prospectors mined
the Granite mountains
and became wealthy.

So too, I have become wealthy
Through your friendship.
I owe you a poem.

I know you are thinking that
I owe you nothing.
Of course, true friends have no debts.
You are right, as usual.

Perhaps I don't owe you a poem.

So, I will gift it to you,
because it pleases me to do so.
Because art recognizes truth.
Because my heart sees your beautiful heart.
Because this is your poem.

19 POEMS from Vero Beach

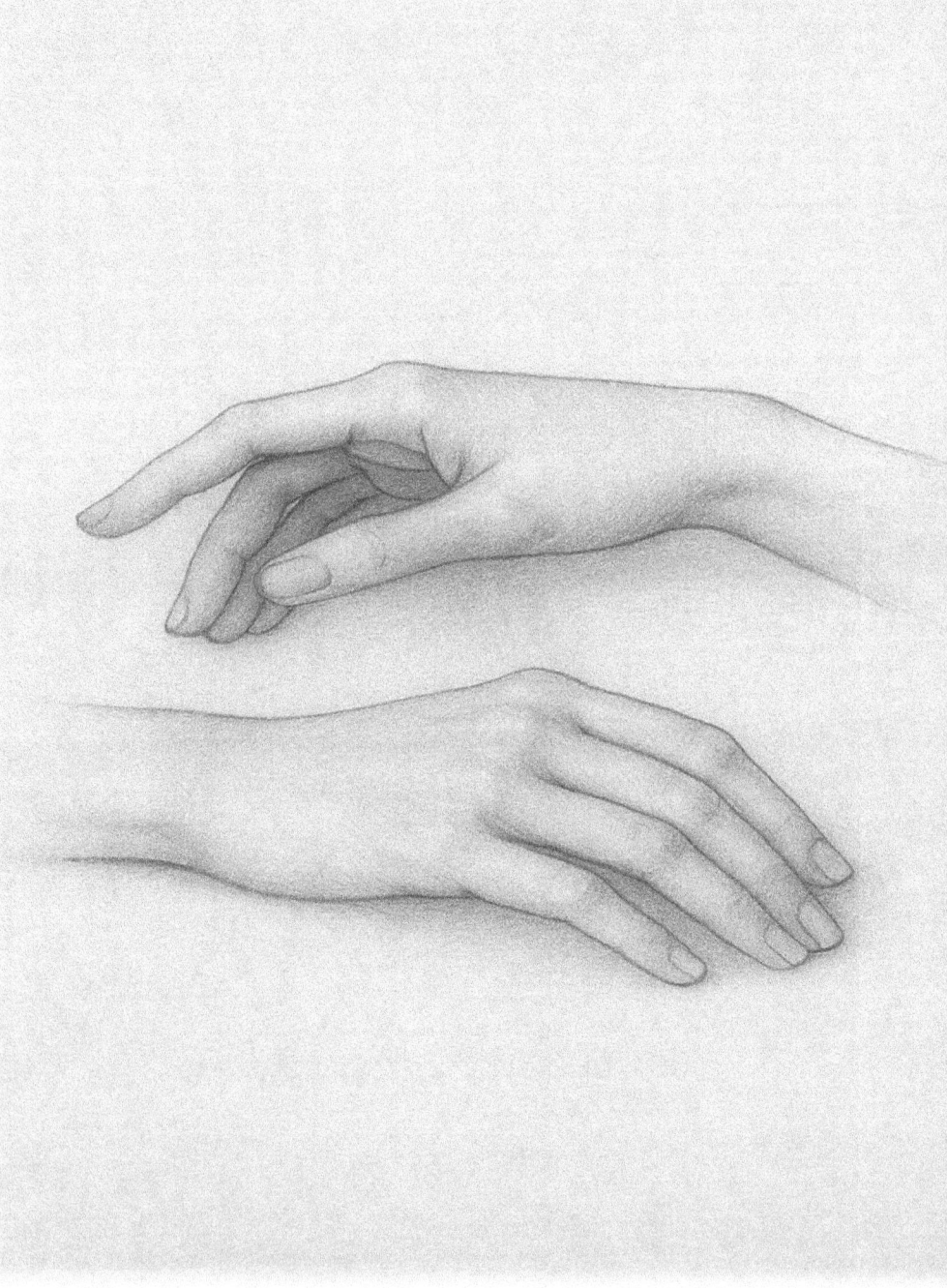

Hands

I stare down at them,
my mother's hands.
The fingers not exactly straight,
curving slightly,
as if refusing to be perfect.

No wrinkles or spots,
just the barely-there, blue shadow
of veins carrying away
their precious cargo.

I see her there.
I see her in me,
as I stare down at my mother's hands.
My hands.
So perfectly like hers,
in my memory.

I ache for my mother's hands.
I wish for just one more touch from them.
I press my hands together tightly,
wishing they were holding her.

She has been gone so long,
but I am never without her.
I see her in my hands,
in my lips,
in my thighs.
I hear her voice as I go through my day,
reminding me to be patient,
to be kind,
to be better.

Anna M. Figueroa

I feel her in my heart
a I stare down at these, my hands.
I squeeze them together in gratitude
for all the times
I felt my mother's hands.

19 POEMS *from Vero Beach*

A Woman Alone

A woman alone, if she isn't careful,
finds herself constantly explaining her solitude.
She must justify her lack of companionship
as if she has somehow
thrown off the rhythm of life's soundtrack
merely by being happy on her own.

"There must be something wrong with her," they whisper.
"Maybe she doesn't like men," they speculate.

I smile as I overhear their theories.
I am too old and too comfortable in my own skin now,
approval as useless as an uncomfortable pair of shoes.

They don't understand, of course.
They don't see that I hoard my peace like a fierce old dragon,
breathing red fire at anyone daring to approach with evil intent.
My time, my love, my passion,
they are the treasure which I protect so jealously with my flames.

In my youth, I gave myself away too easily,
too needy and unsure to take true measure
of the man whom I was gifting.
Fairy tales swirling in my head,
wanting to be loved so desperately,
I didn't understand that he needed to be worthy.
I didn't understand that what I held in my heart was priceless.

Time and pain and disappointment…
they all came and rescued me.
The tears and blood stained the shining pieces of me,
but they did not ruin me.
The water and blood,

like a blessing,
washed away the need and the fear.

I am now free.
Free to give my love without requiring a hero.
Free to receive love without conditions.
Free to love the woman I am.
Free to let myself keep becoming
the woman I'll be tomorrow.

19 POEMS *from Vero Beach*

The Words

Rough, yet so gentle,
your hands on my face.
Your thumb tracing my lips.

"So pretty. So soft."

Hearing you say it
makes me feel that way,
a little.

"What do you want? I need the words love."

The whisper breathed across
my skin makes me shiver.
Such a simple question.
Such a fierce demand.
But no words come.
As I stare up at your wild eyes,
longing seizes me by the throat.
Mute and unmoving,
willing you to pull the words from my lips.
Testing you, even as I deny you.

A crooked smile crosses your mouth
as that wicked thumb
continues its rhythm,
mapping me.
*"Tell me. I won't give you what you want
if you don't give me the words."*

Anger and frustration rise,
as strong and hot as
the awful want inside me.

"I don't have the words…" I protest, like the coward I am.

I stop because we both know it's a lie.
The false words die
in the heat-filled inch
between you and me.
We both know I have the words.
Those brave words you need.
But I'm choking on the fear of
being broken again.

In the end, you win.
The need is greater than the fear.
The love is stronger than my cowardice.

"I want you." I snarl.
"I want everything." I demand. "I want it all with you." I beg.

Tears flood my eyes,
your triumphant smile blurs
as you press into me,
like the rushing waters
through a broken dam.

Giving everything.
Taking everything.
Every damned, little, glorious thing.

19 POEMS *from Vero Beach*

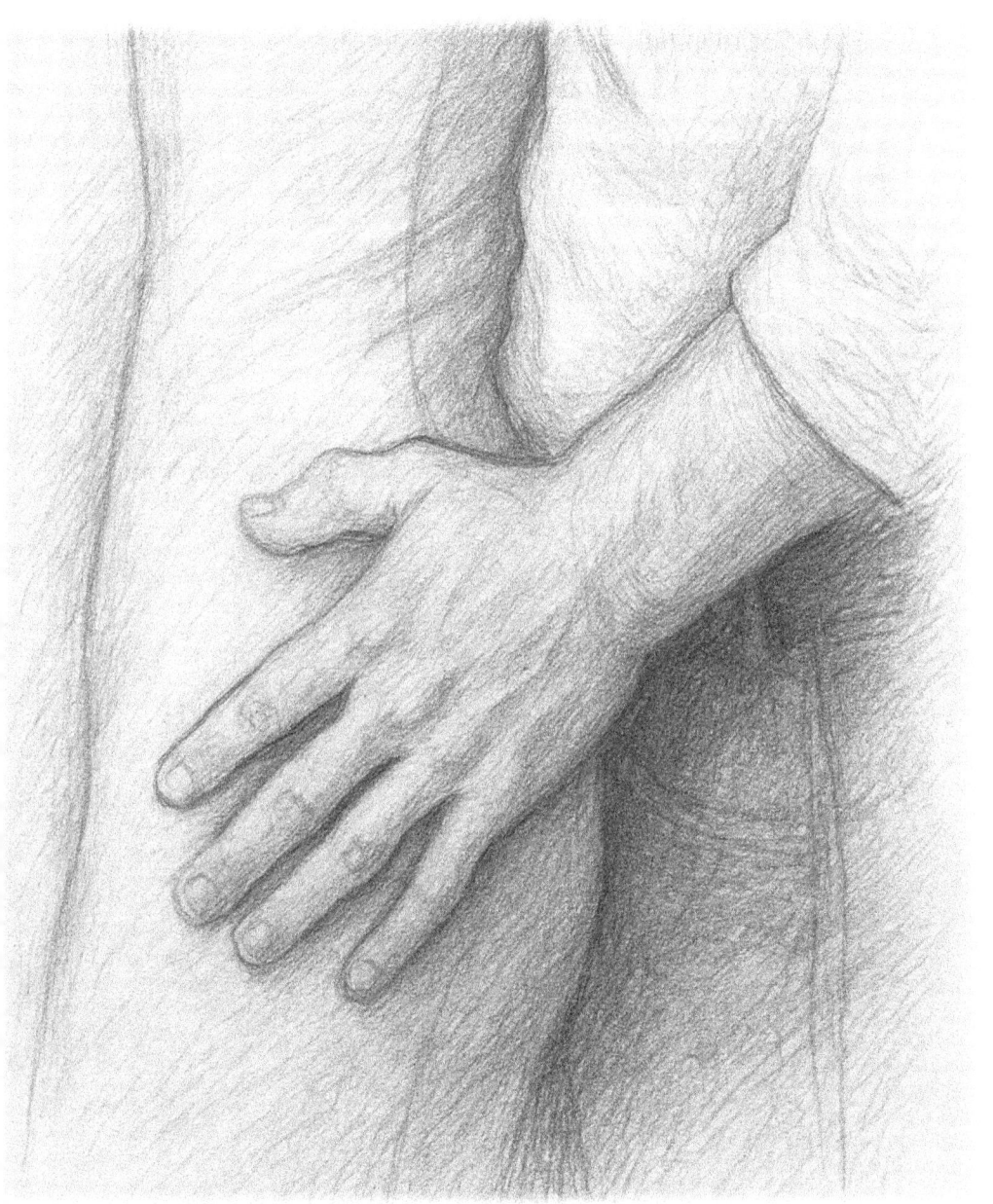

Missed

I missed you today.
That hasn't happened in so long.
It's raining and I'm tired,
so, you snuck in.
I don't know if I miss you,
or just the things we used to do.
Maybe I miss you.
Maybe I just miss your weight
on the mattress as you slipped in beside me,
wrapping around me in the dark.
Maybe I just miss tripping on your work boots in the bedroom.
Or the half-awake coffee in bed on Sunday mornings,
or having your hand on the small of my back.
I don't know if I miss you really.
It's been so long,
I've built another life,
a happy one I think,
but today,
for a moment,
I forgot all the bad and missed you.

19 POEMS *from Vero Beach*

Now

It's time.
Go ahead.
Let your foolish dreams surface
and begin to take shape.
Drown the voices
of those who are too bitter
and afraid
in a sea of wasted time.
It's time.
Go ahead.
What are you waiting for?
Time, though he empathizes,
does not know tender mercy.
He is relentless and just,
passing equally and indifferently
for the sinner and the saint.
He knows only his constant path.
It's time.
Go ahead.
What are you waiting for?
Do you wait for circumstance
or an easy path to things that
only come to you in dreams?
It's laughable, isn't it?
You, sitting here,
waiting on the right time
when there is only time,
with no right or wrong to its essence.
There is only time
and his breath is heavy on your neck.

19 POEMS *from Vero Beach*

All I Am

Stupid girl, believing in twisted villains lurking in the shadows,
and steadfast, savage heroes stepping into the light.
Naive child, believing that rescuing the broken man before her
will give her the elusive happy ending.

Crazy, vengeful harpy screaming out in gut-wrenching pain,
aiming her vicious talons
at the one who broke her
into a million sharp-edged pieces.

Conjuring witch, calling upon the elements
to bring her justice and then magically restore the balance.
Watching the moon shine down,
its cold light upon her angry need.

Exhausted, worn-out warrior,
holding up her dented shield with trembling arms, wondering
what penance she must owe
that she ended up on this bloody battlefield.

Restless, empty woman,
desperate to be seen and to be chosen.
To be chosen...
to be chosen above everyone else.
That's it, isn't it? That right there.
Pick me. Love me. See me. Choose me.

Devout pilgrim, chanting the prayers of her childhood,
seeking the redemption she fears she will not find,
carrying her sins like boulders on her back.

Gentle lover, letting the moonlight kiss her softly,
as she gives all she has inside, all she is,
to the man who saw her truly.

Fierce mother, lioness ready for battle,
so filled with love that she is willing to die, if necessary,
that her children may live and thrive.

Woman grown, understanding
that we are all walking this life together,
fighting our own private wars,
winning and losing,
finding sorrow and then joy.

Stone temple, running water, raging fire, luscious earth and flowing wind.

Spirit and flesh.
Old hag, young maiden.
Mother and daughter.
Sister and friend.
Lover and wife.
Priestess and penitent.
The broken and the healed.

I have been them all. I am still them.

19 POEMS *from Vero Beach*

Love Letters

A woman should never go too long
without getting a love letter.
She will forget her beauty.
A man's words can create gardens
where there were only rocks,
if he chooses them wisely.

To go too long without a love letter
makes a woman forget her power.
A man's words can call
Venus from Olympus down into his bed,
if he chooses his words wisely.

Waiting too long for a love letter
can make a woman's heart brittle.
Too easily she can forget her softness.
A man's words can run
like silk across a warm bed,
if he chooses them wisely.

A woman should never go too long
without getting a love letter.
She will forget the reasons why
she gave her heart away.
A man's words can make love bind
that heart to his forever,
if he chooses them wisely.

Simple, honest words
flowing across paper,
weaving two people together,
reminding a woman that
she is loved and desired,
that she is seen,
make her understand
who her man is.

A woman should never go too long
without a getting a love letter,
lest she lose the girl
that resides in her heart,
the queen that resides in her mind,
and the mage that resides in her soul.

19 POEMS from *Vero Beach*

After

Rocking me like the lazy waves of the morning sea,
your exhausted breath skims across my skin
making me feel drunk.
You smile, because you know what you've done.
Stretching your shaking legs,
pressing into my damp skin,
you remind me,
making me want what you've already given.
Like a marauder,
the weight of you,
above me and around me,
takes everything,
then gifts it back to me.

Unholy man giving me sacred things with a grin.

19 POEMS *from Vero Beach*

Tequila

Tears dragging a black path
of anger and hurt
across her face,
she asked for another.
Shooting it down,
she stared at the sweating glass
as if the answer swirled
in the cold, broken,
shining ice.
She asked for another
and allowed the anger
to rise like a furious phoenix,
out of the ashes of
the pain and rubble left inside,
as she shot it down.
The sound of the glass
hitting the worn wood
exploded like a gunshot.
Something definitely died tonight.
It lay lifeless,
killed by the black, empty,
gaping hole of silence
and bloody carelessness.
She asked for another,
and loosed the rage,
letting it flow free
as she shot it down.
She warmed herself
in its bitter heat,
reminding herself
of who the hell she was.
She asked for another.
The red rage cooled
and she could breathe again,

as she remembered
her name and its meaning.
She shot it down,
mourned her bloodied heart,
and let what had to die
be dead.

***19 POEMS** from Vero Beach*

Woman of Jerusalem

Sandals worn and dusty
from the journey that never ends,
you, proud woman of the holy city,
no longer bow your head.
Mourning, but alive,
finding ways to roll away stones,
your grief and love,
fight for space in your heart.

The awful, beautiful grit of living
has worn your body down
but polished your soul.
Citizen of the holy city,
a place teeming with sinners,
no stones will touch you now.
There is no one to cast them.

You fear they will never know you completely,
afraid that they will forget your name,
making all that you are, disappear forever.

Fierce woman of Jerusalem,
your children's children
will know your name.

Your tears fall
on the dry, cracked earth
of the holy city.
Dry them woman!
For they will sing love songs about you.

Woman of Jerusalem,
the world reaches for your dreams,
eager to rip them apart.
Warrior woman of Jerusalem,
fighting the angry claws
of a bitter place and time
until your last breath.

Raise your eyes to heaven!
For they will sing of your strength and grace.

Drawing the water from the well,
you understood the truth.

Bathed clean, you speak it now.
Oh, what beautiful songs they will sing of you.

19 POEMS *from Vero Beach*

What of You

Eyes bound but opened,
blind still in the cold, dark cave.
The beloved voice calling.
Body and soul reunited,
more than a man,
now a miracle.

What of you?
What of the friendship that ran so deep
that He cried,
mourning you,
even as He gifted you life.

Perhaps they were agonized tears
for all that you would have to bear.
Perhaps they were a glimpse
into the bitter water that would
soon run from Him.

What of you?
Were you shunned?
Were you glorified?
Were you accused of being a fake?
Is the lost ending of
the most privileged of friendships
sitting dusty and hidden?

Did you dream bigger?
Did you go out and live a grand adventure?
How could such a story not continue?

What of you?
Perhaps I am wrong.
Perhaps your story

is written and rewritten,
every day.

What of you?
What of me?
Perhaps we are all Lazarus.

Anna M. Figueroa

The Palestinian

I dined alone tonight.
I drank wine and ate rich food.
I savored it all and tasted the sweetness of the small moment in
my life.

A gentleman came in and sat at the table beside mine,
far enough to remain a stranger,
but close enough to feel his company.
An elderly lady, covered from head to foot sat before him,
a young boy to his right.
He filled the space between us with energy and smiles.

The lady's serious countenance showed first surprise,
then gentility at my smile and greeting.
She said nothing but her face softened,
making her suddenly younger.

He leaned toward me and said,
"Isn't the salad delicious?"
"Yes, it is."
"How is the rest of your dinner?"
"Delicious, and yours?"
"Wonderful!"
"Bon appétit!"

We returned to our meals,
feeling somehow fuller.

The course over, the next placed before me,
he leaned over to me again.
"Do you live here?"
"Yes, sometimes."
"Sometimes?"
"I live here, and I also live in Miami."

He knew a little about my city.

Again, he leaned.
"Are you Italian?"
"No, I am Cuban. Where are you from?"
A momentary pause, his face more serious.
"Palestine."

What does a Cuban American woman from Miami say to a Palestinian man living in a sleepy beach town?
It was my turn to lean.
"I'm sorry for what is happening. Is your family ok?"
"So far."
Looking down, he said quietly,
"My food gives me less pleasure now. They have none."

"My people also have none."

The silence between us is heavy with understanding.

I leaned over and said, "I pray it ends for everyone soon."

He gave me a sad smile and answered, "I pray it ends for your people too."

I felt the need to add, "Don't lose the pleasure of your meal. You are here, with your family. Grab happiness when it comes."

His smile became brighter as he nodded.

Warmth in our eyes, we turned back to the plates, and glasses, and the beautiful food before us.

19 POEMS from Vero Beach

Fly

So, I close my eyes, and I fly,
to a world that unfurls before me,
showing off voluptuous curves,
defiantly owning its terrible, dark corners,
so much like a woman who has lived too much,
for too long,
but who still knows love when she sees it.

I am free here,
free to be myself.
Here, on the streets of yet another, unknown city,
released from the bonds of routine and expectation,
liberated from my own anxious thoughts,
by the beauty of ancient bridges
and imposing castles,
rough cobbled streets, and high-speed trains.
Here, I become the explorer,
the adventurer,
and discovery brings such joy.

I embrace it all,
what enchants,
and what repulses,
knowing that I am now richer,
deeper, freer.

The world offers up its smells,
its tastes, and its textures.
So I feast.
I let myself fall in love with the pink sky
shimmering in the noisy fountains,
like champagne.
I celebrate the dreamer
locked deep inside me,

quietly letting her escape,
if only for a moment.

Anna M. Figueroa

19 POEMS from Vero Beach

Through the Smoke

The white gray swirls,
circling and winding around me,
a heavy fog that makes me fight for breath.
Through it, I catch a glimpse
of something that used to be.
Pin pricks dancing on the tip of my tongue.
The ghost escapes me,
taunting me to chase it.

Through the smoke,
shadows and silhouettes swaying to the music
that somebody else is playing.
Where did my notes scatter to?
Where did my heartbeat land as they fell?
I recall a fragment of a melody
and it cuts like a cruel shard
as I try to remember the words.

Desperate, I begin to hum.
The smoke shifts,
agitated and disturbed.
What were the words?
Anxious, I try to wave the smoke away.
I need to see.
I need to see what's beyond the haze.

Where there is smoke, there is fire.
Isn't that what they say?
Then why is it so damned cold?
I hum harder,
thinking that the words will clear the air,
making the notes return and my heartbeat again.

Words matter.

Their weight so great that
they are as bricks that can build
or knock down fortresses.

Through the smoke,
feral, yellow eyes stare,
trying to distract me
from the words I need.

Straining, humming,
breathing in the smoke,
I search for the words.

They will tell the story.
They will reveal the truth.
They will make me real again.

Anna M. Figueroa

***19 POEMS** from Vero Beach*

Unwritten

I sit in the fading light,
swirling the amber in my glass.
As I watch it dance,
all the unwritten poems inside
shift and rearrange themselves.

The silken words of love,
the acid words of betrayal,
the gentle words of faith,
the terrible battle cries of the warrior,
all rattle around inside me,
vying for my attention.

I don't wish to jumble them all.
Words are sacred and
shouldn't be spewed carelessly
nor dropped like wayward, rolling dice.

Their stories are rooted
in holy ground,
I'll not trample them
because I'm restless.
So, the unwritten
will stay that way tonight.

I'll finish my scotch
and lay down,
hoping that the words
turn into dreams
that remind me of who I am.

19 POEMS *from Vero Beach*

Stay with You (for Enzo)

I hold you gently in my arms,
feeling your soft warmth,
breathing in your innocence.

My thoughts all rush towards one truth.
I want to stay with you.
Always.
I can't, but how I wish I could.

Oh, how I wish to see all the beautiful colors
you will splash across your sky!
How I hope to watch joys of your life unfold!
I'd give anything to see the look on your sweet face
as you delight in the magic of the world!

I want to stay in the world with you
so that I can see all its enchantment
and sorrow through your eyes.
I want to fall in love with it all again,
because your very existence makes it
more tragic and more beautiful.

I want to stay in the world,
so that I can celebrate your valiant choices,
and wipe the tears from your face
when life and people let you down.
I want to stay with you,
through every hard-won victory,
through every vicious heartbreak.
It will all happen, with or without me, won't it?

I want to stay… of course, I can't.
I will rage against Time as long as I can,
but we both know that Time will win.

But no matter, my beloved boy,
though never long enough,
what a glorious time we will have together!
How I treasure every moment, every smile,
every sweet, soft breath of your sleep.

My heart fractures, thinking that one day,
you might not remember me.
But no matter what, for every day of your life,
for every treasured second,
while I stay and when I go…
know that on this earth and then later,
in whatever heaven waits for me,
I will be watching over you,
thinking of you,
and loving you.

Since you've been a good sport,

here are a few more from

other places and moments...

Being

The grey creeps through the sky
above me, around me, in me.
Uncertain if to offer welcome
or withdraw in fear,
I press back into the creaking rocker,
matching my tempo to the thunder.
I test my memory for the rhythm.
The rhythm of timeless rain,
of mothers and lovers.
It comes to me slowly,
dancing to the rumble and light,
above me, around me, in me.
With it comes the familiar ache,
as timeless as water,
rolling from the leaves,
to drop like tears to the earth.
The wet wind soothes me,
giving the ache substance,
until the grey and the rumbles,
and the damp wind,
wake my senses
from their hammered dullness,
returning them to the earth
like children to their mother's arms.
My eyes no longer see fragments,
as the circle takes shape and meaning.
For a moment, I understand that I must be still
if I wish to move forward. That I must be silent,
if I wish to truly speak.
That I must be wind and rain and thunder,
if I wish to be a woman.

Anna M. Figueroa

Not Forever

I cannot promise you forever,
I don't know that it exists.
I can promise you truth,
whether it brings joy or loss.
I can promise you my eyes,
looking straight into yours,
not down or away.
I can promise you my mouth,
open for your bitter-sweet taste.
I can promise you that,
with your touch,
my sea will rise and break
on your shore.
That after that shattering violence,
you will know the peace
of lying in my depths.
I can promise you that in our anger,
I will stay and fight,
and spit fire, rather than leave
in a coward's silence.
Silence that dresses certainty
in the shroud of doubt,
withering and drying the heart.
I can promise you laughter,
so free and true,
that it will wash us clean
of the world's stains.
I can promise you that
when I pray to God,
from the center of my soul,
I will beg for your happiness.
I can promise you that
when the pain arrives,

It will not outweigh
the wholeness of us.

19 POEMS *from Vero Beach*

Anna M. Figueroa

Midnight

As the curious yellow moon peers down,
I strain to find words of revelation.
In the silence of the dim night,
I reach for hidden truths.
Twisting and turning the words,
I whisper them to the stars,
Marveling at the momentary meaning.
I look to myself in the words,
written in lonely darkness.
For as I unveil their hidden forms,
I discover my unfamiliar shape.
With each revealing phrase,
I gain texture and weight,
Growing, changing,
As truth releases.

Anna M. Figueroa

19 POEMS from Vero Beach

Julio's Stride

Will you remember,
the lazy rays of light leading the tiny, dancing specks
in the hall between our rooms?
Will the smell of coffee and just-sliced apples
remind you of our silly, rushed mornings?
As you answer the echo from the distant horizon,
and begin to carve your mark on the face of the earth,
will you remember the great, majestic dragons
we conquered together?
When you love the women
who will choose to love you,
will you hold them more tightly and reverently
to your heart when you think of me?
Feel no sadness as you go,
for your leaving is slow and,
though painful,
fills me with pride and wonder.
For you are more than I,
as I too was once more.
But on the way,
as you walk through what you are destined to create…
Remember me.

September 1996

19 POEMS *from Vero Beach*

R&B

She sat alone in shadow, a smile turned still,
Staring across the house, remembering.
The horn played scratches, accompanied by horns.
The yellow turned rose and scented the air with newness.
It seemed so long a trip from the deep chair.
The stage and lights behind
The mist of years.
The time to sing once more.
The last.

19 POEMS *from Vero Beach*

Autumn

It is cooler here now.
The air is crisp and sharp.
The sky, clear as polished glass,
is a blue so brilliant
as to seem stroked by an artist's hand.
So many colors,
a riot of bloody reds, happy yellows,
warm oranges and brittle browns.
The indigo sky pays homage
to the green that remains,
in spite of the season and its changes.
Was I color blind before?
Will I see the colors again?
In spring, I believed in beauty,
but did not understand its fleeting nature.
In summer, I had no time
and too much arrogance to see.
So I rejoice in my autumn,
in the coolness of my breath,
the clearness of my vision,
the strong beat of my heart,
as the whispers of the world
vibrate through it.

19 POEMS *from Vero Beach*

New Orleans

With the glowing ruby of the evening sky
came the slow, brassy music
of a thousand unseen horns in the night.
The mysterious dusk swirled to the melody
and circled, wrapping itself around you.

I saw the hovering moon bend low
to kiss your open mouth.
In my jealousy, I shut my eyes…
only to hear the roughness of your love
whispered over my tightening throat.

You brought the music inside me,
making it seem my own,
timeless rhythm.

As we danced that night,
the sweet fragrance of gardenias
mingled with the burning glide of old brandy,
the urgent moon spent her caresses,
the dusk waltzed into the distance,
the ruby cooled to deepest onyx,
and on tangled sheets,
under an open window,
my New Orleans was born.

Gently

So gently you left me.
At first, there was nothing
but the brush of your cheek,
still warm, against mine.

I did not believe it possible,
that you could be taken so quietly,
still encircled in my arms.

But like the drunk, sobered against his will,
I could not pretend.
The agony of your absence
burns constant,
light that gives no warmth,
pain that allows no rest.

So gently you left me.
In death, your words of love fell softly
on the breast that so briefly,
for so achingly brief a time,
gave you life and comfort.

I could not keep you.
My screams and tears would not,
could not,
return you to me.
I, who so often protected you,
could do nothing but love
as so gently you left me.

Anna M. Figueroa

19 POEMS from Vero Beach

Rage for Silence

There is no silence where I am.
Always the sounds,
within and without,
intrude and invade,
leaving no place for peace.

Like the novice equestrian
pulling in terror on the cutting reins
of an unbroken stallion,
I scramble to block out the noise,
trying to keep my precarious balance.

The beast knows me not,
nor does it seem familiar.
The only certain knowledge
is that we both wish
to occupy the same space.
Each willing to fight to the death
for ultimate possession.

The battle waged is unfair,
one-sided and costly.
The enemy invades easily,
yet its fortress appears impenetrable.
Despair pierces my flesh
and I bleed in great red gushes.
My soldiers tire,
their armor heavy and dented.

So I pray for deliverance
with each clash of the sword,
as the clanging and smoke of the battle
meld with the dull, unending roar

of the hated invader's
breath on my face.

19 POEMS *from Vero Beach*

Twilight Dance

Into the light, I turn
so that you might see me
through the glass.
If I stare long enough,
will you see beyond me
to what I want?
I spin again,
as restless as the fan
that brushes my body
with warm, empty air.
It torments my damp skin
with its pleading whine.
I press my hands together
to keep them from
caressing your absence.
Around me,
the house responds,
creaking and shifting
like a nervous voyeur.
How does a woman
take a man
where she's never been?
How to seduce
from such a distance?
I shift to the glass once more
to find feverish eyes staring.
They close and again, I circle,
nails sinking deep.
I reach for a glass
to wash down the bitter taste
of another night alone.
The fan stirs the static air,
the house watches and mourns,

I turn and bow
to the desperate music
of solitude.

19 POEMS *from Vero Beach*

Chasing Shade

There, in the chasing shade,
truth races forward,
ever hopeful,
forcing jagged confessions
through chinks and fissures.

Relentless hunter,
leaning down upon its prey,
it closes in,
inevitable and inexorable,
seductive.

In the darkness, no lies.
Time and shape and movement
mock all,
reducing the effort
to flat black.

So it chases and caresses,
issuing the undeniable invitation,
bare and empty,
that alone leaves space
for new life.
So desired, so feared.

Y porque soy hija de cubanos...

Tres de la Tarde en la Ciudad (Sentada, Esperando las Cinco)

Quiero que se me arrebate la soledad,
que se me arranque la noche vacía
de este pecho triste y pálido.

Quiero ser besada,
y quemarme como espada acabada de forjar.
Quiero ver las luces que solo brillan
detrás de ojos cerrados,
sentir la caricia de un respiro escondido
en la oscuridad de mi cuello desnudo
y besar los dedos de un secreto.

Quiero ser besada,
doblada por el dolor de un amor que rompe
lo que vivo y lo que dejo de vivir,
sacudiendo lo que espera en silencio.
Quiero abrazar el misterio del atardecer
que pasa, aunque yo no esté,
susurrando mi nombre mientras se va,
triste y cansado de esperarme.

Quiero ser besada
parada en las sombras de una puerta abierta,
ahogándome de las ansias, vigilando,
mientras la brisa de la noche sin estrellas
hace arder mi desesperado sentir.
Quiero el alivio divino
de la última sombra de la tarde
que cruza y entra en mi temblor.

Quiero ser besada,
probarme en la boca del que me besa,

cambiarme en su sabor.
Quiero besar el cielo en el hombro de mi amante,
morder un sueño distante,
tragar la luna blanca,
beber el sol de primavera
y dormir regada en una cama extraña.

Quiero ser besada...
a las tres, de la tarde en la ciudad...
(Sentada, esperando las cinco.)

19 POEMS *from Vero Beach*

19 POEMS *from Vero Beach*

Nos Queda

Nos queda…

La magia de una palabra en un momento preciso,
cambiando de órbita los planetas
para siempre.

El sonido de las teclas del piano,
subiendo, bajando,
rompiendo y callando.

El espacio entre el alma y la conciencia,
imposible de navegar premeditadamente,
cruzado inesperadamente
en un enfrentamiento interno.

La sombra de las pestañas de mi hijo,
enmarcando sus ojos tiernos,
acariciando sus mejillas.

El instante en que dos se entienden,
solo con el toque de sus miradas,
penetrantes y cálidas.

El vibrar de la sangre pulsando en mis venas,
bailando al ritmo elegante
de nuestro amor.

Anna M. Figueroa

19 POEMS *from Vero Beach*

Mi Poder

No te puedo prometer la eternidad,
no me convenzo de su existencia.

Te puedo prometer la verdad,
aunque traiga con ella perdida.

Te puedo prometer mis ojos,
mirando los tuyos,
sin esconderse en rincones imaginarios,
esquivándote.

Te prometo mi boca,
abierta, saboreando tu amarga dulzura.

Te prometo que, al tocarme,
sentirás mi mar subir y romper
sobre ti.

Que, después de esa violencia,
suspendido en lo más profundo de mí,
conocerás mi paz.

Prometo que, en nuestras diferencias,
Me quedaré peleando
En vez de escaparme en el silencio del cobarde.
Silencio que marchita y seca el corazón.

Te prometo una risa
tan libre y sincera,
que nos limpiara de las manchas del mundo.

Te prometo que cuando venga la oscuridad,
rogaré por tu felicidad.

Te puedo prometer que
cuando llegue el dolor,
no borrara nuestra verdad.

19 POEMS *from Vero Beach*

LA HABANA

Vieja ciudad, tan bella y tan terrible.
Cápsula del tiempo mal sellada;
la sal, la humedad y la separación te comieron de adentro hacia afuera,
derrumbaron lo que parecía eterno.
Vieja, misteriosa ciudad, llena de historias y de mentiras,
de ilusiones y de vacíos, de héroes y de villanos.
Tu historia no se ha acabado de escribir.
Como una mujer bella quien, al no encontrar un buen amor,
envejeció descuidada y gris de la tristeza.
Te encuentras abriéndole la puerta al extraño,
quien viene a curiosear tus leyendas.
La Habana, ciudad dorada y olvidada,
tu gente sueña con lo que fuiste
y con lo que pudieras ser,
acá y allá, allá y acá.
Sueñan tus hijos con noventa millas de mar,
con lo que deben saborear en tus calles y no pueden.
Sueñan con dejarte, sin saber que se pasarán el resto de sus vidas soñándote.
La Habana, ciudad deseada como un dulce,
elegante a pesar de tus tenderas y extranjeros.
Tus edificios son los huesos más bellos del mundo.
La Habana, ciudad irreal que vives en la memoria de todo cubano,
hasta la de los que nunca han caminado tu malecón.
La Habana, donde todo era mejor
y dicen que todo mejorara... algún día.
La Habana, donde nuestros padres dejaron sus ilusiones
y nuestras madres dejaron su juventud.
La Habana, donde nuestros abuelos fueron felices,
hasta que te hicieron transformada en una ciudad desconocida
y violenta.
La Habana, cuna de tanto dolor.

La sol, tu brisa y tus palmeras acarician a mis seres queridos,
cuyos fantasmas sus sombras los mantienen alejados.
Pero eres la preferida del mar,
eres amada, eres llorada,
la más recordada y añorada por la libertad.
Por eso eres y serás venerada,
la ciudad de la patria libre y renovada.
Tus calles se llenarán de la alegría de tus hijos
quienes solo soñarán con quedarse en tu cálido abrazo.

19 POEMS *from Vero Beach*

Cuando te Vayas

Cuando te vayas,
lleva contigo el perfume de mi pelo
cuando de suave cortina servía,
para esconder nuestros besos.
Como seda se deslizaba,
cayendo como mis caricias sobre ti.

Cuando te vayas,
lleva contigo la medida de mi cintura,
memorizada por tus brazos que la atrapaban
mientras lavaba platos olvidados por ti
en tu mañana de prisas y luchas.

Cuando te vayas,
lleva contigo la marca de mis dientes
en tu hombro sudado,
ya que solo tú desbordabas
ese volcán en mí,
violento y primitivo,
nacido de mi pasión por ti.

Cuando te vayas,
lleva contigo mi mirada,
ya que en mis sueños
te seguiré contemplando.
La misma mirada que
en su día era suficiente
para calmarte o encenderte.

Cuando te vayas,
lleva contigo mi corazón,
ya que de nada me sirve.
Guárdalo con las pocas
caras y cartas que tengas

de tus amores ya distantes,
para que cuando te encuentres solo,
o cansado, o herido,
de algo sirva el amor de esta mujer.

Caída

En la ternura de mis senos,
olvidaras tu cansancio.
Mordiendo la curva de mi cintura,
vengaras tus derrotas.
Entre mis sólidos brazos,
recuperaras tu niñez.
Entre mis piernas suaves y cómodas,
serás victorioso.
En los rincones de mi corazón,
alcanzaras tu sueño de ser héroe.

ABOUT THE AUTHOR

Anna M. Figueroa lives and writes from Miami, Florida, where she blends her rich life experience with a deep commitment to storytelling that resonates. As a mother, entrepreneur and breast-cancer survivor, she has forged a path marked by resilience, reinvention and the bold decision to give voice to the complexities of women's lives. (Amazon)

Anna's writing is grounded in lived reality: she brings the streets of Miami, the pulse of her Cuban roots and the universal experience of womanhood into sharp focus. Whether writing in English or Spanish, she invites readers into characters who dare to stretch beyond what's comfortable, to embrace change, to own their voice and their story. As she herself has said in her blog, "our strength is not determined by our rigidity, but rather by our ability to grow and to stretch and to evolve." (Midnight Thoughts)

With each book, Anna M. Figueroa draws upon her own history—of survival and transformation—and offers up stories that are intimate yet expansive, rooted yet reaching for possibility. Readers will find in her novels both the familiar and the unexpected, the challenge and the hope, and women who are not afraid to ask: Who will I be, now that I've become myself?

www.ingramcontent.com/pod-product-compliance
Lightning Source LLC
LaVergne TN
LVHW051246080426
835513LV00016B/1769